Hymn Favorites

Table Of Contents

Cover photograph courtesy of Erwin and Frances Towne. The Old Towne Grove Chapel is located in Groveland Illinois and is a quarter scale model of the 160 year old St. Pauls Lutheran Church in Madison Illinois.

Exclusive Distributor - J.T. Publications / Heartland Music Inc.

The Chords Used In This Book

The following chords and progressions are those used in this book. It may enhance your playing ability if you practice and memorize them in both their sustained and broken forms.

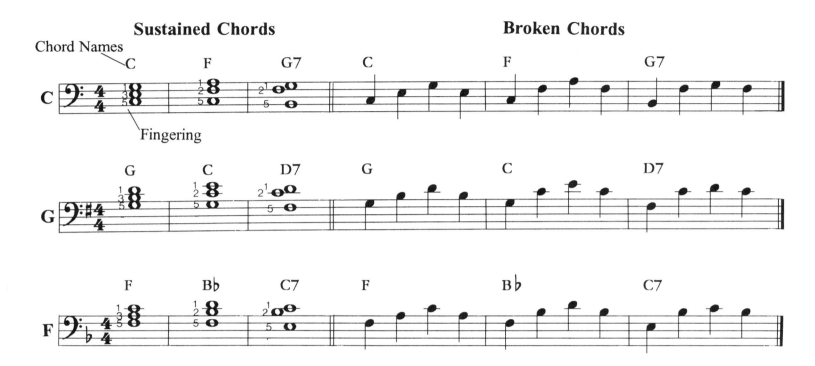

Basic Chart Of Note And Rest Values

Notes	Rests
Whole Note	Whole Rest
Equals	Equals
2 Half Notes	2 Half Rests
Equals	Equals
4 Quarter Notes	4 Quarter Rests
Equals	Equals
8 Eighth Notes	8 Eighth Rests
Equals	Equals
16 Sixteenth Notes	16 Sixteenth Rests

Signs

♯ sharp

♭ flat

♮ natural

⌢ fermata

staccato

stress

accent

𝑥 double sharp

𝄫 double flat

strong accent

first and second endings

triplet

C (common time)
4 beats to a measure, quarter note gets one count 4/4

¢ (alla breve)
2 strong beats to the measure, half note gets one count. 2/2

repeat sign

tied notes

slurred notes

8va octave

Abide With Me

W.H. Monk

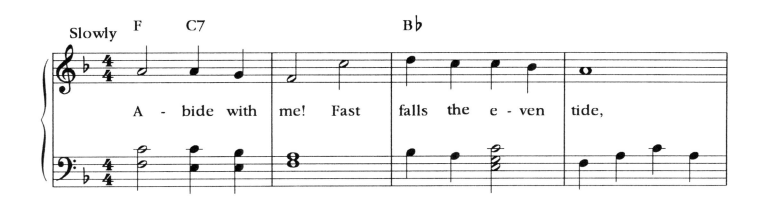

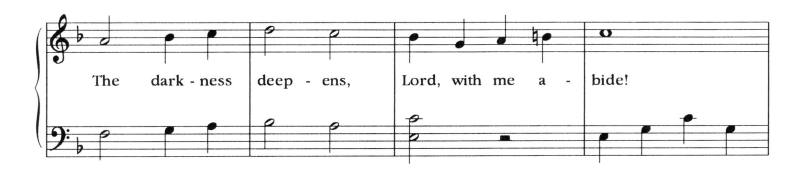

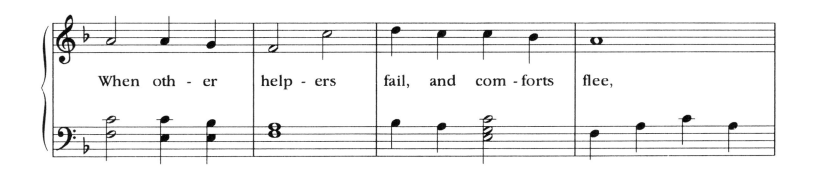

Amazing Grace

Traditional

Bringing In the Sheaves

Shaw-Minor

Give Me That Old Time Religion

Traditional

He's Got The Whole World In His Hands

Traditional

Hallelujah, He Is Risen

(Easter)

P.R. Bliss

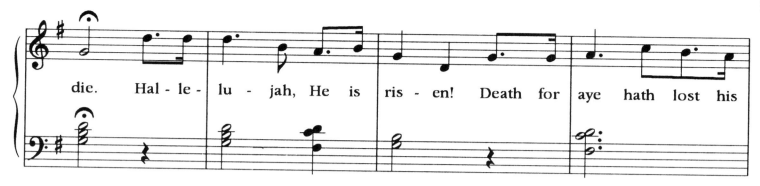

die. Hal - le - lu - jah, He is ris - en! Death for aye hath lost his

sting, Christ, Him - self the Re - sur - rec - tion, From the grace His own will

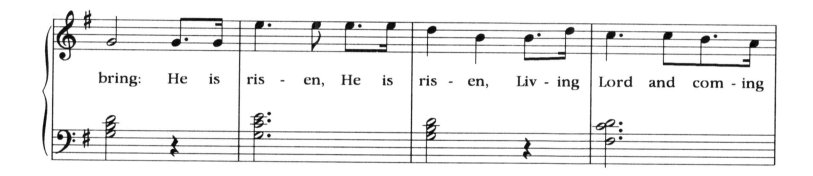

bring: He is ris - en, He is ris - en, Liv - ing Lord and com - ing

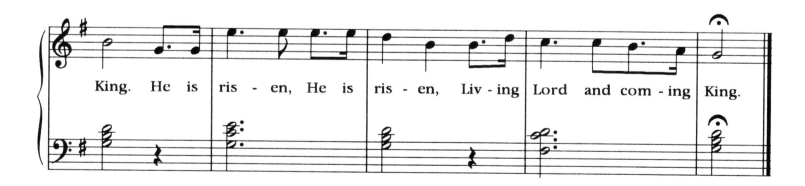

King. He is ris - en, He is ris - en, Liv - ing Lord and com - ing King.

The Holy City

Weatherly - Adams

In The Sweet By And By

Bennett-Webster

Jesus Loves Me

Warner - Bradbury

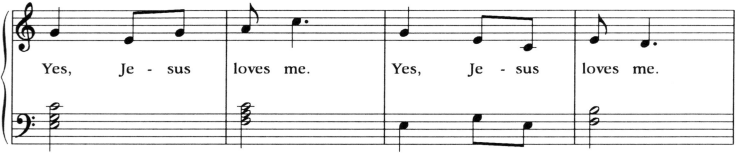

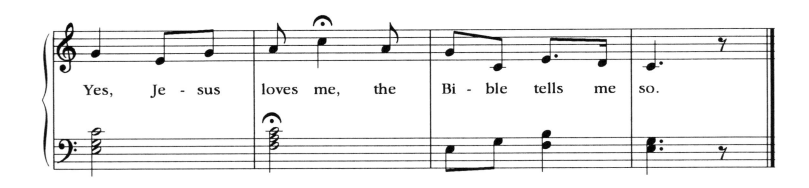

Kum Bah Yah

Nigerian Religious Song

Just A Closer Walk With Thee

15

Morning Has Broken

Lyrics: Eleanor Farjeon
Music: Traditional

Nearer, My God, To Thee

Adams-Mason

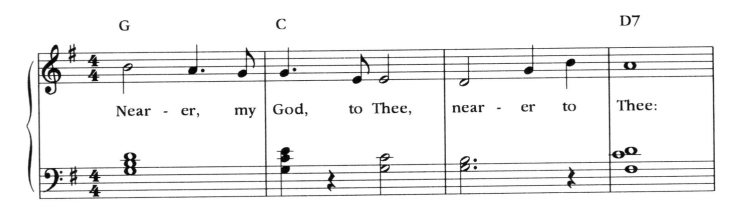

Now Thank We All Our God

(Thanksgiving)

Rinkart - Cruger

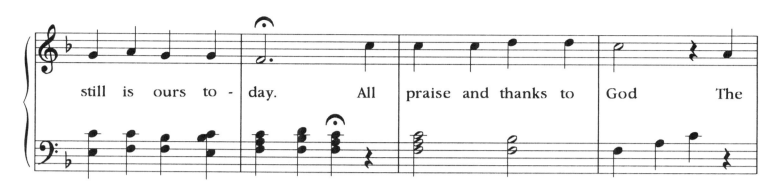

still is ours to - day.　　All　praise and thanks to　God　The

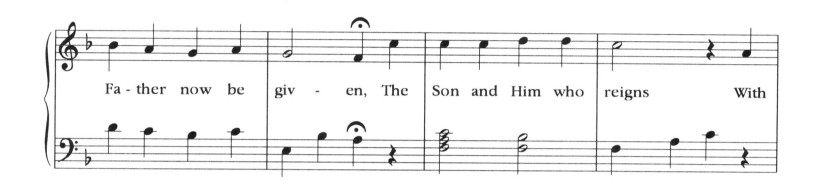

Fa - ther now be - giv - en, The Son and Him who reigns With

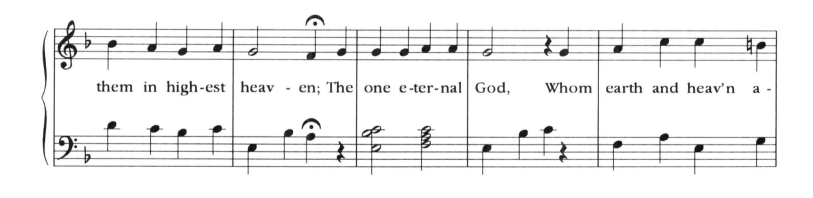

them in high-est heav - en; The one e-ter-nal God, Whom earth and heav'n a -

dore;　For thus it was, is now,　And shall be ev-er more.

Nobody Knows The Trouble I've Seen

Spiritual

No-bod-y knows the trou-ble I've seen, Glo-ry, Hal-le-lu-jah!

Rock Of Ages

Toplady-Hastings

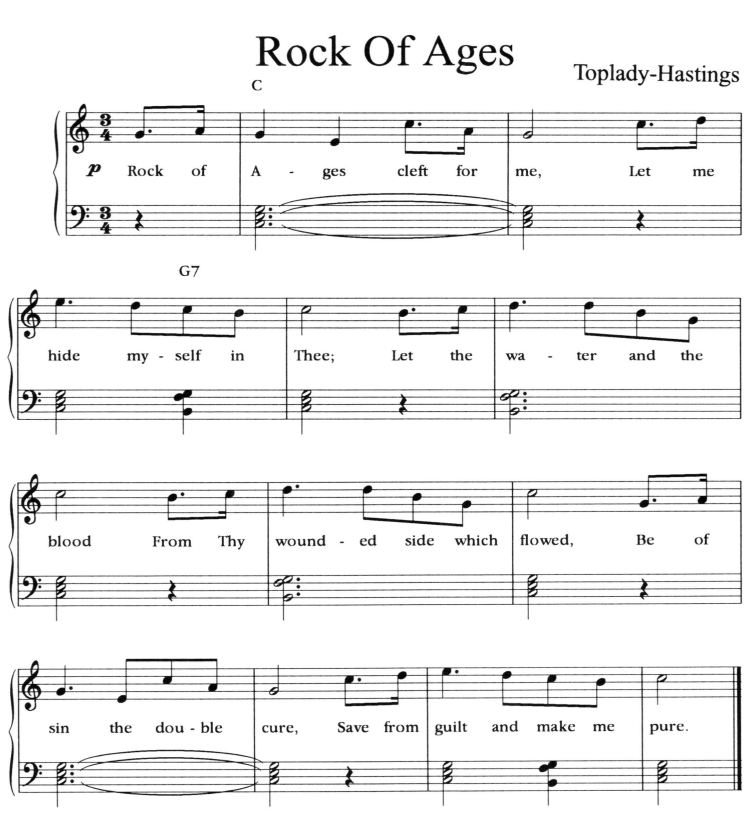

Rock of A-ges cleft for me, Let me

hide my-self in Thee; Let the wa-ter and the

blood From Thy wound-ed side which flowed, Be of

sin the dou-ble cure, Save from guilt and make me pure.

The Palms

J.Faure

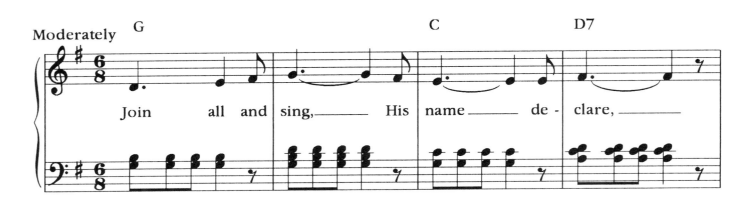

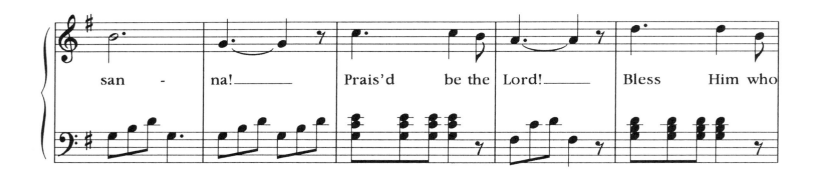

Swing Low, Sweet Chariot

Spiritual

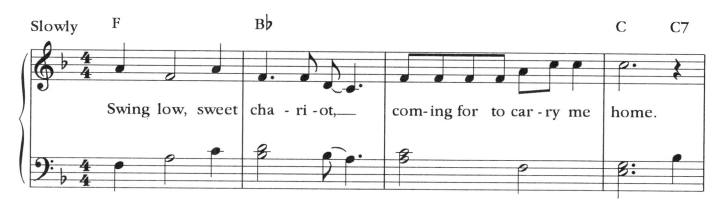

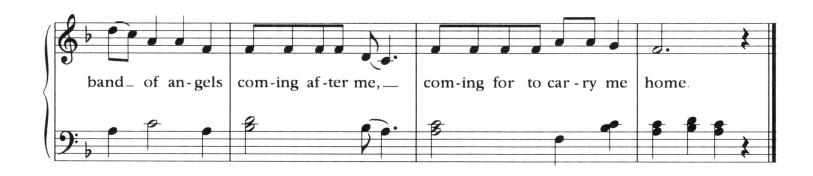

The Rosary

Rogers - Nevin

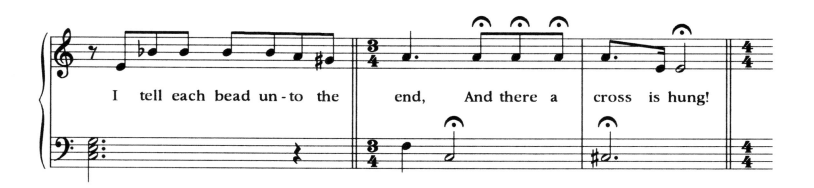

I tell each bead un-to the end, And there a cross is hung!

O, mem-o-ries that bless and burn! O, bar-ren gain and bit-ter

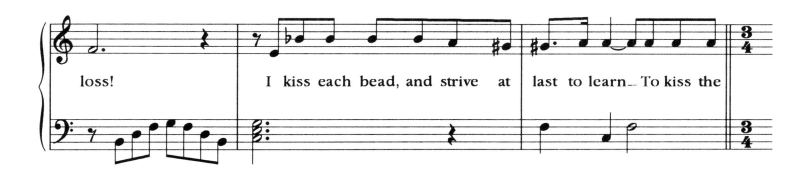

loss! I kiss each bead, and strive at last to learn— To kiss the

Cross, sweet-heart! To kiss the Cross.

Standin' In The Need Of Prayer

Spiritual

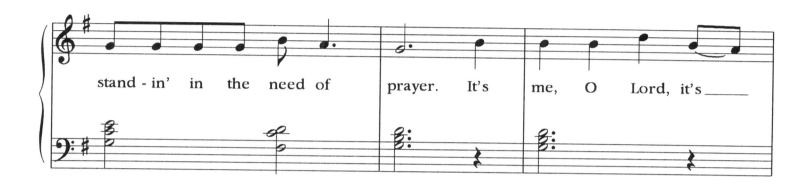

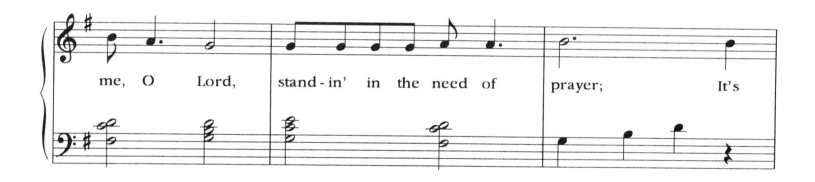

Whispering Hope

Hawthorne

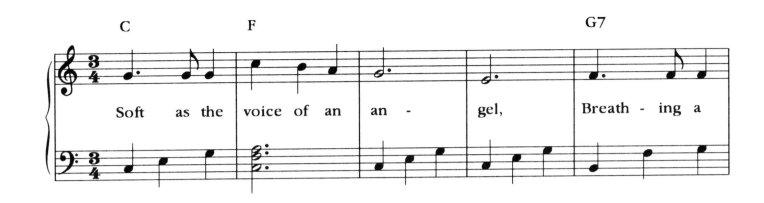

Soft as the voice of an an - gel, Breath - ing a

les - son un - heard,_____ Hope with a gen - tle per - sua -

sion, Whis - pers her com - fort - ing word:_____

Wait till the dark - ness is o - ver, Wait till the

What A Friend We Have In Jesus

Scriven - Converse

Wonderful Words Of Life

P.R. Bliss

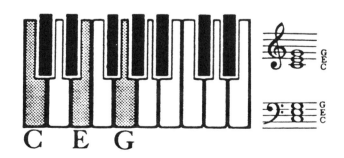